To Bob,

I hope that you enjoy these poems

Kind regards

John

Last Word

John Murray

Pen Press

First published in Great Britain by Pen Press

All paper used in the printing of this book has been made from
wood grown in managed, sustainable forests.

ISBN13: 978-1-907172-41-0

Printed and bound in the UK
Pen Press is an imprint of Indepenpress Publishing Limited
25 Eastern Place
Brighton
BN2 1GJ

A catalogue record of this book is available from
the British Library

Cover design by Jacqueline Abromeit

*My wife Jo has been a wonderfully
understanding, tolerant and patient collaborator
and I both thank her warmly and dedicate this
collection of poems to her.*

Author's note

This third collection of poems journeys through the seasons in the unique physical environment of the Var in southern France. It also continues to explore the ever-absorbing nature of relationships between men and women. Finally it turns towards the later stages of life both in celebration of the journey so far and in anticipation of its end.

John Murray
Seillans, 2009

Contents

Varois Seasons

Men and Women

Mortality

Varois Seasons

*The Var is the most heavily-wooded department in
France, a steep and stony region of vertiginous gorges,
gushing flood waters, searing heat, scrub, oak and pine.*

*Its tough brown people are close to the land, clearing
ditches, growing, tending and harvesting vines, cork and
olives, cutting wood, mending stone walls, tending sheep
and killing the ubiquitous wild pigs.*

*Thunderstorms assail the arid summer months, the
Mistral regularly scours the hills and winter brings deep
daily frosts in this savage, unforgiving terrain.*

*But the light steals the heart each rose-tinted morning
and golden evening, while kites and ravens wheel all day
in the uniquely blue sky.*

New Year's Night

Harsh frosts coat each blade
of grass in deep mid-winter nights,
lawn appears a glistening cake made
by surreptitious hands. Noiseless flights
of owls glide over silent grounds
stilling frozen field-mice,
distantly heard, the mournful sounds
of watchdogs, left outside to brave the ice.

The New Year coldly steals the Old
while sleepers warmly dream. Cold,
cold the early dawn, starlit, still,
Venus staring bright above the chill.
The Old Year topples to its death.
The New begins with icy breath.
The cold, the stars, the owls, the frost
proclaim another year is lost.

February gale

Morning wakes the hills, shutters clattering,
mistral bares the soughing trees and gusts
round walls with blustering battering
force. Early light, blue and bright
behind a sunlit moon. Too soon
to tell if rainclouds will swell
into a stormy morn.

The day awakes, stretches, shakes,
remembering there's a world to oversee
before returning dark. It takes
its time, the sun begins its climb,
mistral at its heels, then hovers, wheels
and points towards the west. The air feels
bruised and torn.

Evening. Fireflies in the hills, the lights
of hamlets, resting from the wind, the nights
a haven from the tiring gales of Spring.

Spring

Spring is the conventional time
for hearts to lift, for brown to turn to green
for women to conceive,
bringing fresh-born hope to those bereaved
in winter, when glistening rime
furs the barren twigs and unseen
spirits hang icicles on graveyard gates.

But this year my heart will not thaw.
I contemplate a world at war,
young men filled with hate
and I remain in winter.

Late Spring

The oak trees know.
They watchfully observe the April surge,
the pushing shoots and smile, the urge
defied to greenly grow.

The hills hold snow.
Cherries pinkly flaunt their flowers,
but in the night the frosty killing hours
will see their vaunting slow.

Frogs protest their willingness to mate at any price
but spawn is dying in the late Spring ice
and magpies raid the nests
of early doves.

Forsythias gaily, madly
boast the birth of Spring, a flimsy claim
of yellow life, their blossoms all the same
change hue, die sadly.

Wysteria coyly wraps
its buds in fur, ready to retract
or to respond to sun, defences packed
against cold wintry snaps.

Firesmoke scent
in evening air. A robin's trill
wistfully repeating, hopeful still
that winter will relent.

Summer storms

A screech of jets rips through morning air.
I spot them just in time, a steely javelin pair
in military grey, carving a parabola of skill
on wing edge silhouetted on the hill.

They disappear, tearing shock-waves fade.
The mountains stir, their rocky sleep is shaken;
now they grumble, mumble, groans relayed
from older peaks to younger as they waken
a chorus of dismay, echoing those nights
in summer when vicious violent lightning lights
a blackened sky and sheeting rain attacks
these hills where rolling thunder cracks
and bellows angrily.

The rocks take up the roar
passing the message round in savage glee,
escalating monstrous noise, an atavistic war
destined for eternity.

Summer breeze

Mistral streaming, brightness gleaming, mountains
newly scoured, fresh-empowered to greyly oversee
the blueness blinding over winding swollen streams
which meet and greet the white-blown sea.

Tossing birds, soundless words, tugging sails, wind
in every face, the pace too much, taking the breath,
stealing all feeling save for wild elation at the danger
bravely met, feet set apart forestalling falling.

A violent gust inspires the dust to scatter, whipping
windows, lashing hulls, flinging gulls high
above a seething bay. They stay aloft, wildly squalling
in excited fear, trusting on a gust to steer them down.

Buffeting ears, it veers to land, looking north for
home. The foaming sea begins to calm,
to ease. A breeze is all that's left, scant evidence
of the gale. It's over. A flagpole clanks its thanks.

Summer sleep

Float in the pool
lazy and cool,
lavender humming,
bees coming
and going.

Birdless trees
windless air
smooth brown knees
combless hair,
mulberry shade
just made
for favourite wine
with a favourite friend,
occasional murmur
at the edge of sleep,
that sweet afternoon sleep
of summer.

November

The vine can only wait.
Loved for twenty years,
now comes its brutal fate.
The driver slowly steers
close by, bends to chain
the helpless stock,
and feels the wicked pain
of deicide, a shock,
remorse at terminating life
so gladly given for the God of Wine.

His chain takes up the slack, the strife
begins, resistance, but the engine's whine
can only have one ending.
Surrendering, the light-starved roots
see hills at last, bending
to the tractor's will, free
of their grave of clay,
they view their day
of liberation and of death.

Destined for firewood, only good
for burning, no more turning
sun to grapes, their gnarled shapes
tiredly say goodbye.

Wintry weather

Spinning leaves and pelting rain,
cold disheartening December.
Shall we ever feel again
the late gold summer of September?

Rain-soaked limbs of oak are battered,
sliding tiles, a crash of shattered
terracotta.
Broken dreams of sunny summer
lie in shards,
pool-drenched days, cicadas
scratching sleepy afternoons.

December day, sodden clay,
the muddy mess of winter
underfoot, I hold
a jagged splinter
of a potter's pride
at my side
and yearn
for life to return,
in Spring

The wolves of Mercantour

You have to go quite high, into the snow-line,
if you want to feel that prickling spine
when the long howls start late at night.

It is mountainous up here and dark,
forget the so-called national park,
this land is wild and bony-white,
containing memories of fear,
rapid shadows moving near,
stolen children, stifled screams,
grey shapes leaping swollen streams
and waiting at the hamlet gate
for travellers returning late.

Shepherds lying with their sheep
try to cope without their sleep.

Confident of their powers
they pass the daylight hours
in sleep, then stretch and whine and growl,
then gather up the pack and howl,
fear pulsing down the rocky scree.

The guardian dogs prick up their ears
but only see their masters' fears.

Christmas is coming

It's coming up Christmas
I can tell.
No lights or bunting
but hell,
why am I humming carols?

It's coming up Christmas
I can tell.
Robins tick on every twig
when I dig
and turn the earth before the frost.

It's coming up Christmas
I can tell.
The pool is full of leaves,
mice rustle in the eaves
and I'm thinking of logs.

It's coming up Christmas
I can tell.
I hear the village bell
tolling out the year.
Oh dear,
another year.

Men and Women

*The love-sickness afflicting the young
is replaced in later life by a more knowing,
more complicated and often an ambivalent
and compromised vision of love, while the
detachment of age endows us with a stronger
perspicacity about the imperfections
which are a feature of most relationships.*

*Equally as time gets shorter we sometimes develop
a restless impatience with the similarity of days
and seek to extend the boundaries within which
time and convention bind us.*

Young again

She came to me last night
skipping past a lifetime
to take me by the arm
and look into my eyes
again, at last.

She came to me last night
eyes brimming with the joy
of youth and took my arm
and we were young
again, at last

She came to me last night.
Her look of love pierced me
through and there was nothing
in her gaze but me
again, at last.

Then she left,
my sweet young love,
left me alone
yearning for the past.

Pointless

I loved her so so much,
her urgent want-you glance
squeezing the breath from my heart.

We didn't keep in touch
after she wed.
Pointless, when romance
is dead.

Many years have passed,
but every day we meet;
stout ladies with glasses,
grey hair, in the street
or in a shop.

I never stop
or say hello,
to my lovely girl of long ago.

Her smile

Hard to refind
the sheer vigour of youth,
when sleep was an option
rarely exercised.

Tough to recapture
that madness of love,
that thirst for her presence
never satisfied.

Sad to recall
laughing young days,
that time before irony
damaged our hearts
and cynicism warped
our souls forever.

But sometimes her smile
recalls for me
those lovely days
when we were young.

Manly thoughts

Men think of little else
and women know it.
That's why they close their knees
when sitting, or sometimes not.
They penetrate your mind,
seeking your essence.
Men think of thighs
but girls look in your eyes
and evaluate.

You're being measured all the time
and not your inside leg.
They are looking for truth,
checking that impulsive youth
has gone and that what is left
is kind and wise.
So they look in your eyes.

Wives

They listen while he boasts
of his undoubted but
exaggerated talent.

They tolerate his sense
of self-importance, so
pathetically misplaced.

They harken to his views
and hear his insistence upon
how the world should be.

They patiently endure
his psychosomatic fears,
his endless vanity.

They watch him roam
the room, looking for a
pretty face to entertain.

They offer him their bed
from time to time, just to
stop him wandering.

They say they love him.
But despite their virtues,
sometimes wives
don't tell the truth.

35

Hands off

I'm getting lonely
becoming sad
need her nearby
need a soft hand
to stroke my face.

I want to hear her say
that she will always stay
nearby to stroke my face
when I need her hand
to stop me feeling sad
or lonely,
say she will
never never leave
me lonely unstroked
or sad.

But now I am ill,
now I'm truly unwell
don't want her
hand on me,
nobody nearby
just face the wall
that's all
I want.
Just leave me
all of you,
leave me alone.

Falling again...

Here he comes,
shaking off his last
conversation, new
interest in his eyes
as he spots my face.

He has seen it all,
my clothes, my hair,
my shoes and legs,
quick-fire evaluation,
years of practice.

But most of all
he has seen me,
deep into me
where my desires
lie hidden.
Only seconds yet
he knows me well.

I must fight him,
but I can already feel
the familiar pain
of heartbreak as I
fall in love again…

...triste

I have dreamed of this,
that you would be lying
in my arms, eyes lost in mine.

I have thought of this,
your warm breath sighing
in my ear, your skin divine.

We lie together
just as I foresaw,
just as I had hoped.

But now I must tell you
this is nothing new,
there is nothing different.

We have been here before
and it ends the same way.
So do you want to say
goodbye,
or shall I?

Don't ask

Don't ask me now to stand
beside you, nor hold your hand;
nor comfort you. Nor share
your dreams.

Don't ask me if I love you.

I am here.

Just let it be.

Remembering

Women remember all too well,
hoarding events of years long past,
sustaining feuds so that they last
until their source is dry
as dust and just
as insubstantial.

We are long past the thrill
of it all, toothless husks
in baggy pants, paying still
for those days when we were men.
We had the strength back then
to make our little world resound
and women gathered round
to see us clash our tusks.

But is the cautious feeble gait
of these once masters of their fate
not revenge enough?
Do not the snores and farts
and ailing parts
sufficiently humiliate?

Have we not paid the price?

45

Staying the course

Do you recall that evening air sublime
when glow-worms lit our path to perfumed sleep,
the ocean washing at the bone-white sand
below the terrace where you held my hand
and said you loved me?

Where did it go, my dearest girl?
We didn't see it leave, but it has gone
and left us trusting we can stay on course,
against the odds, without recourse
to bitterness.

Trying to be kind

I really raised my game today,
an effort to refind the way
it used to be.

No sharp-edged barbs, no sighs, no glares
and when she disagreed no stares
of incredulity.

When she trespassed on my space
I didn't bark or pull my face.
I listened while she voiced again
those views I've known since way back when.

I think she rather liked it.

Truth to tell, it was
easier for me too.

Week off

I swing the car north
leaving the airport,
farewell to stress,
already glorying
in freedom..

She has gone.

But next week I am back
standing off the crowd
waiting to spot her
determinedly making
her way back to me.

I can think
of worse fates.

My girl friends

I have a quite extensive list
of women I have never kissed
but whom I love and they love me
and when we meet our eyes are lit
with tender warmth, complicity
in guiltless happy love.

Although these girls are not my wife
and seldom feature in my life
I share their palpable delight
in warm and hugging amity,
in feminine felicity,
treasuring my place
in their unqualified affections.

Sometimes one can almost see
the pleasures of sorority.

Trade-off

Would you give your life for hers?
Would you gift her all you own?
Can you grant her deepest wish,
do you truly want to please,
is your sole objective just
to serve unquestioning?

No, it isn't, is it?
Of course not.

And so the bargaining begins,
your pure love diluted
at once by grim negotiation.

But it takes two to tango,
or would you rather not dance,
milady?

Cross my heart

I've thought about our years
together,
including tears
and stormy weather
and wondered if
a kinder gentler man
would not have made
you more content,
you the country maid
and he the perfect gent.

But I have my doubts.

We are the sum of our parts.
Our hearts
are inter-twined forever.

I love you still, never
fear, my dear.
If you should die
before me
I shall cry
for eternity.

Pussy

Feeling stressed?
Need a break?

The best place to go is somewhere slow,
a place that knows not cold nor snow,
a calming place
that gives you space
to dream and contemplate.

No need for palms on sea-washed shore,
nor huts with sea-shells round the door,
no bracing walk
on cliffs of chalk,
just room to mend, recuperate.

I found it, not too far away
and now I go there every day
and stroke her golden hair
as she lies within my arms

(everyone should have a cat).

Girls in Cannes

Mexico was not for me,
not at all my cup of tea
with all those begging cheeky boys,
the traffic and the endless noise,
the self-obsession of the men,
that sudden awful moment when
Montezuma introduced himself.

No, give me Cannes any day;
it's nothing like so far away;
you can drink the water, park your car
and the girls are prettier by far,
what with no moustaches
and so on.

Not yet

Don't talk to me of love,
I'm bored already.
Don't tell me that romance
has flown.
That's known.

Don't tell me of my faults,
that I'm unsteady
or no longer want to dance
with you.
It's true.

Don't say my heart is cold.
That story's told.
No second chance,
we can't retract
a fact.

But, please don't say
let's call it a day
or let's get ready
soon to part.

Let's try another year,
my dear,
my dearest heart.

Mortality

…the paths of glory lead but to the grave (Thomas Gray)

Black and blue

Folded in a darkening heart
lie silent intimations of
the end of life.

But we won't think of that today
nor speak those words that say
our time is short.

We will muse instead on blue,
on bright blue skies,
your dark blue eyes.

We will ponder Homer's sea,
its treasures sunk invisibly
beneath the swelling blue-green waves
in darkest depths, in deepest lands,
the work of Attic sculpting hands,
sea-soaked in their graves.

Drowned Aphrodite, Eros' staring gaze,
unseen works in Neptune's dim-lit rooms,
his gallery in the Middle-Sea.

But, if blue does not amuse you,
we will go back
to black.

No friends today

I called today but it's no use;
he is turning off the lights,
pulling out the plugs of friendship
as he prepares to die.

I tried elsewhere, another friend,
but quite in vain.
His ass was in a ditch
or some such tired excuse.

I spoke to God, but he was vague,
pre-occupied elsewhere;
they are all the same,
fine weather friends.

So finally I turned to Hell.
They put me straight through.
'Right, what shall we do?'
asked the sin-stained voice
of Satan.

Fear

Dark is all right,
even at night
on a moonless track.
I don't mind black.

Solitude's fine.
I don't really pine
when nobody's there.
I don't really care.

Worry and stress,
I have to confess
I thrive on the kick.

Aching and sick
is less easy to bear
but I cope with my share.

No, what I really fear
is to be misjudged,
to be misunderstood.

Chapelle de Sainte Roseline

Well, yes, the Chagall mosaic is just
superbly evocative, the angels, the bread,
the shock of colour amidst the dust
of the chapel. If you like instead
Giacometti's brutality that is there too,
not to mention Brea's bright stained-glass
and of course the Saint herself, lying
black-skinned on her back, feet
pointing heavenwards, eyeless. A few
dead roses, beads, nothing too crass,
in fact some minutes at her side and dying
doesn't seem so daunting.
Later on you meet her eyes,
in a container on a wall,
meaningless, grotesque,
but above all
haunting.

Ancient Templier spirits hover in the beams.
The sleeping Priestess folds them in her dreams.

Mary

It isn't hard to lose a friend,
just ask the vet.
His needle quickly brings the end.
All over, yet
your sorrow
barely started.

Broken-hearted.

You hope tomorrow
you will throw it off and smile
but it will take a while.

A lifetime in fact.

Raven

A wall of limestone at my back
I lie and watch a speck of black
above the cliff,
broadly circling in the blue,
crossing a vapour-trail or two.
Its wings are stiff,
maybe a kite,
turning slowly in the light,
buoyed above the greying ledge
of ancient stone, sharp edge
etched upon a deep blue sky.

This seems the perfect place to die,
soul ascending, flying
over peaks and plains,
relieved of care, of worldly pains,
weightless, soaring, no more sighing,
over broken dreams or shattered love,
sailing high above
the crying.

The raven speaks,
a desolate croak
then slides away.

Morning

Changeless Normandy, cream-white
cattle stilled in Orne-banked mist.
Ghostly eucalyptus poles,
bleached stems stark in stands of
darkest pine.

We drive on by,
towards our fate.
The trees watch us,
waiting to enchant
our successors
in their misty morn,
this silent dawn.

A tentative sun strives to wake
this ancient dreaming land.

Grievance

Some times the words can't do their job,
they can't express the depth of grief,
the deep-felt hurt can't be defrayed,
the bitter taste of good betrayed.

Your endless self-analysis,
the constant replay of the facts,
a sense of gross duplicity
augment and magnify,
heaping pain upon affront.

It just won't go, it's just too deep
you can't forgive, you cannot sleep.

But listen….
life is long
and any wrong
will fade away
if you just say
it's all OK,
forget it.

So come on,
be a good chap,
forget it.

Facing it

I haven't yet had time to choose,
still thinking.
I'm going to do it when I can,
heart-sinking
feeling that I'll lack the nerve,
keep drinking
and hope that it will disappear.

I want to be a man
and face it,
do it today,
not turn away
but somehow I
just cannot find
the courage.

War

Born when England held its breath
midst air-raids, absent men and death,
I watched the pain of war assault
bereaved bystanders, free of fault,
my aunts amongst them.

It seems few lessons have been learned.
We must conclude that frequent war
fulfils a fundamental need.

It is nonetheless
painful, bad,
hateful, mad,
destructive of the human spirit
and of uncles.

Going together

I left a letter with the bank
explaining all the money stuff
so it should not be too tough
for the children to figure,
but what an inconvenience
going together this way!

There were so many links
I wanted to play
and she would have
liked to have seen
her grandson grow
from small to tall,
to have been
there for him.

I hadn't even bought a grave.

The truck driver was also killed
but at least his wife will
have the pleasure
of her grandson.

I just hope the police didn't steal
my wallet. You can't trust anybody
these days.

87

Death in the countryside

Sudden swerve to miss the bird,
screech, beech, smash, crash,
then steaming silence.
Not a word.

Beaters tap birds through the wood
up to where the guns are stood
lethally patient on their pegs
black dogs poised beside their legs.

Spaniel's nose disturbs the briar,
pheasant up and soaring higher
sailing on fixed wings but then
crumpling at the Purdey crack;
a gundog briskly brings her back,
mortally punished for her sin.

An ambulance brings the bodies in.

Give generously

We've been there, banking on wing-tip
into Kai Tak, splitting an airpath through
the washing, hordes of humans in the grip
of squalor, wearily oblivious to
our deafening arrival.

We've seen it, the shanty town
at Merida, beside the runways, corrugated
iron their walls, squatting down
like flies in clouds of kerosene, fated,
their only goal survival.

We've smelt it, the stench of death
in Kabila, skulls and thigh-bones neatly
ranged, lethal proof, their dying breath
still unavenged, the West still sweetly
unconcerned.

Dying on Sumatra's shore,
derailed train in Bangalore,
rampant Aids on mud-hut floor,
can't respire any more;
to me it looks the same,
no-one to blame,
just our old friend Death
passing by.

White tie,
charity ball,
publicly write the cheque, that's all.
Rolex visibly on wrist,
couple of thousand won't be missed,
tax deductible, suck the cigar,
pick up the phone, order the car.
Sorted.

Young swimmers

Gold-limbed bodies glisten in water
splashing and diving, somebody's daughter
and her friend;
with untamed grace
they turn and race
rose-flushed cheeks,
the girlish shrieks,
of children far too young for men.

Then
I see them lying in the street,
bloodied arms, no legs, the blast
of bombs signalling last
moments for sweet
young girls, golden hair
begrimed with dirt,
guts agape through tattered shirt,
lying there
like uncollected refuse.

Murder, dressed as war.

Black moustaches

I'm slowly confirming a radical view
that all mankind's problems are principally due
to black moustaches.

You are going to ask me who?

Lenin, Engels, Hirohito,
Castro, Hussein, Marshall Tito,
Guavara, Stalin, Mussolini,
Hitler, Marx, Signor Martini
(the rifle, not the drink)
That's what I think…

…need I go on?

Weakening

The rich are getting younger,
all energy and hunger
for goals we never even glimpsed.
But that's alright.
It really is alright.

Ambition dribbles weakly
down, its absent force meekly
faced,
replaced
by sagacity,
a long-headed capacity
to remember and
to see round corners.

That's about it, I'm afraid,
not very impressive.
We were not always so useless,
though weariness conspires
with weakness so to make it seem.

Perhaps we will be remembered?

Not for very long, I suspect.

97

Pickwick to the rescue

I crouch in my corner
peering through the bars
of insecurity.

Waiting for something,
something bad
to happen.

Trying to gauge what
enormity would so oppress
me that I would not want
to live.

I can envisage it,
but I cannot tell you.

But if it happens, I think
I will refresh my spirit
by re-reading Pickwick Papers.

Then I will review the situation.

Invisible

The day I fall
and breathe my last
you will all
walk past,
suddenly struck blind
as death comes calling.

As you see me falling
you will smartly cross the street
suddenly pull out your phone,
adopt your special business tone
and ask a nearby client to meet,
detaching yourself from
this embarrassing occurrence.

The rest of you will step aside
pretending that I have not died
here in the street,
right under your feet.

It's true.
Go on, admit it.

A pity, but that's the way
things stand just now.

Funeral odes

I spoke at his funeral.

Did she wonder
if the words were true,
from my heart,
or just a patter?
Was I playing a part?
Did she feel
that it was real?
For that matter,
did I ?

There is a surefire way to tell.
When hot tears well
and you lose your voice,
you have made your choice
and declared your love
for him.

Last word

From time to time I promise
I will kill myself.

I'm not sure how or even why
or if I'll have the nerve to try
but illness, grief, regrets and
longing sometimes aggregate
into an immense ganglion of
dissatisfaction,
imploring the relief
of excision.

So here I stand contemplating
the loss of life to come.

But, not for the first time,
cowardice has the last word.

Late Quartet

1. 'I'm very sorry, but…'

They've seen a bit of shit,
a lot of gore,
these grey tiles
on the clinic floor.

They stare at me,
wordless
and I stare back,
struck dumb.

His words spell
out my fate,
the knock-out bell.

It's getting late.
Time to go home.
I know the drill,
check through the will.

She holds my hand
trying to understand
the shock, as the clock
starts to count me out.

2. Drinks afterwards at the house…

No need to smother me in pity,
please don't 'sorry' me and whinge
and please don't let me see you cringe
when I approach, the shitty
stench of death fresh on my coat.

It's been a hard few hours,
painful for us all
and thank you for the flowers,
though I doubt if you will call,
or even send a note

when I really need you.

But never mind,
drink up, my lads,
sup up,
down the hatch,
cheers,
here's
to life,
what's left of it.

Great chap, good man,
what a shame, blah, blah.
My, don't we all
enjoy a good funeral!

(I'll cry later when
I do the washing-up).

3. Buried last week…

Seventeen unanswered mails,
indecipherable scrawls,
statements, bills, renewals, calls
he would have dealt with, all
wait unattended,
at an un-manned desk.

How can I adjust a boiler,
clear a drain, repair a wall,
work a chainsaw, prune a fruit tree,
how will I survive, is all
I can think of.

Who will help me with my crossword,
who is going to mend my pearls,
how to know which shares need shifting,
who will do the heavy lifting,
all his paperwork needs sifting,
I can feel my spirit drifting
spiralling down, hopelessly
fatally down.

I'll just say this once,
I need my man,
my lovely man.

4. Obituary.

So you used to be a sportsman?
A man and his ball.
Is that all?

And you used to read a bit.
Oh, great.
Is that it?

And do the crossword
on the train.
What a brain!

And wear a suit in meetings,
the handshakes and the greetings
at your Club.

You knew your wine?
Oh, fine.
And you liked to shoot?
Rooty-toot-toot.

Not a lot to show,
but no second go,
old boy.

Your obituary makes
thin reading.

End